# Coagulated Memories

First Printing, 2022

ISBN Paperback 978-0-6456424-1-4

ISBN Hardcover 978-0-6456424-2-1

Ebook ISBN: 978-0-6456424-0-7

Katri Maree

Australia

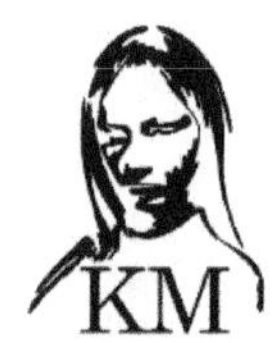

*A Coming of Age Collection of Poetry, Prose and Illustrations*

# Coagulated Memories

Katri Maree

# CAUTIONARY NOTICE FOR VULNERABLE HEARTS

"This book contains references to alcohol consumption, sexual assault, abuse, mental health topics of anxiety, depression, self-harm and suicide ideation."

For those who hurt me, those who saved me,
those who ignored me and those who didn't
know at all.

With thanks to my husband.
Without you I am nothing. I am
forever grateful to you for loving
me as I am, and saving me from
myself.

To that one person… communication would
have been the easier option.

They ask, "Would your younger self be happy with what you have achieved in life?" I know my younger self; never saw too far into the future to know what she wanted. She probably never imagined her painful days would be shared publicly. I do believe she would be upset with me, but then again, I'm just finishing what she started…

# INTRODUCTION

I would often write to release emotions of my experiences. Struggling with the pressures of childhood and coming of age; and challenges of who I was, who I wanted to be and who I was expected to be. I was propelled into emotional chaos. This book is a collection of poems written during those dark times.

It took twenty years to open up and be vulnerable, collate my diaries and regress into the memories of trauma to produce this book. My teenage self would be shocked to see that what she created through her painful days would be one day turned into a book.

It is common for people to struggle with sharing their hardships, emotions, weaknesses and creativity. It feels daunting and revealing and obviously a fear of rejection usually hinders progress. Going through my diaries felt like I was that young girl again. It was also nice to see it through my current eyes, older and wiser, able to understand myself.  It was a tough process, and it is just as hard to share.

Teenage Poetry is important. It is a glimpse into the mind, emotions and struggles of a crucial developmental period in life. While other people may not have related at the time, it was very real to me and I felt ignored. I want this book to bring awareness and to also help people who may be coping with relatable issues.

One thing I've come to realise is my personality over time has changed very little. I have always been sensitive to emotions and enjoyed playing with expressing ideas creatively. During my tough days I learned to dissociate from my emotions, therefore I felt neither dead nor alive. I was lost for so long. I decided it was time to come back to the living. Perhaps it was my age, rested emotional state, or the recent current events for this new found clarity?

I am an artist of emotional expression. I am obligated to share myself, or I am not myself. I must not hide any more.

Katri

iv

Deep Breath...

# <u>Table of Contents</u>

xii

PART 1

# Teen Years

*A coming of age thriller, laced with gas lighting and a lack of resolution.*

2

## Cold Nights

A silent room full of screams

She sits within her mind

A whisper of hope echoes through the bars

This prison she claims as home

Drowning in tears

No one exists here

Empty faces with cold black eyes

The chains embrace

Feeling safe

Her world, her thoughts

Dying in morbid dreams

Living in macabre lies

The candle still burns inevitably

Just as the soul, sleeps innocently

Until another dawning day

When the dead arise and dance again

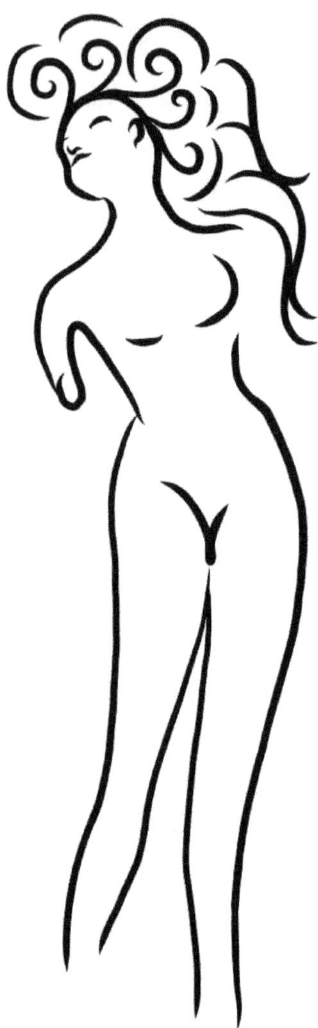

Damaspia

# Dehumanise

Predacious gaze of hate poetics
Watering down cheap cosmetics
Hatred in his soulless eyes
Timeworn grease and extra fries
Stale beer breath and plastic meat
Endorsing dreams of self-defeat
Crowded room of desolation
Fading into contemplation

## Epitome of Reputation

Lavish life of dirty sheets

Visible flesh and filling the script

Tarot card condemnation

Loathing carved in constellation

Vacant hearts and empty friendship

Dreaming of fame and expecting worship

Lottery prize, 9 months' probation

Deteriorating rapidly past expiration

Cigarettes and blaring pistols

Showing off your bag of crystals

## Existence

Seventeen years old, afraid to rest, to close my
eyes and food ingest.
Carefree exterior, chaotic within. Routine and
avoidance, guard paper thin skin.

I drank to be social, I ate large or I starved.
Dressed for expression, hiding scars of the
carved.

Observing from corners. Writing poems all night.
Creating artwork all day, slept by TV light.

Always felt lost, that people endure me. Paranoid
one move, they will exclude me.

Staring through my walls, tearing me apart,
reading my soul, devouring my heart.

I found my saviour in music, tunes filling my
veins, aesthetics, artistry, lyrical stains.

I felt connected, understood me complete, I felt
powerful, hopeful, future concrete.

The pain of my sadness, confusion of heart,

loneliness accepted, my life, my art.

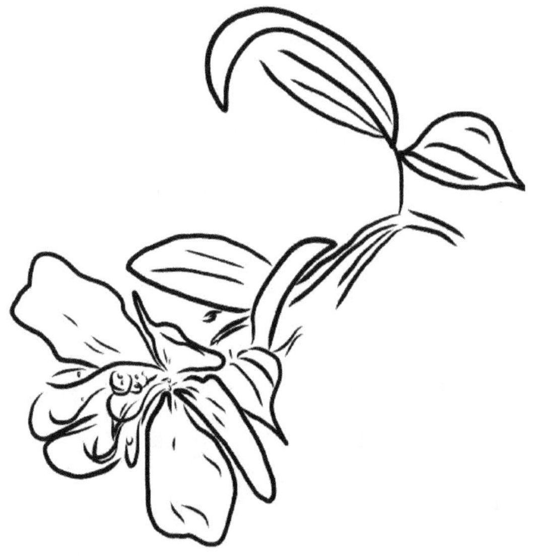

Life

## The Abattoir

Desolate lives dwell behind the doors,

Inside the walls of contention.

Evident suffering,

Muted screams of abhorrent love intention?

Mutinous spirits persisting.

Tears of the morbid child.

Death taken nest.

Rotted corpse a distant dream.

I wait, watching, breathing, beating,

Decomposing, amongst the living,

I am immortal.

## Smile makers

Raindrops in summer, and laughs that don't end.

Music and movies, chats with a friend.

Boyfriends and chocolate, silver heart rings.

These are but few of my favourite things.

# Freedom

They enjoy pointing out my faults,
Telling me how I must be.
They hate the things I feel sure about,
The things that define me.
They reward the things I question,
The things I don't care to be.
No matter how hard I try,
I'll never be free.

12

## Trauma

Midnight she screams

As the living sleep

Stronger as the night goes on

Thinking, creating, Learning and loving

Everything vibrant, clear and pure

Desiring sunrise never to born

Yet the Final Gestation

An ending of dreams

She rises as the days before

Amnesia of the night

Becoming a new being

Walking the daylight

An imitation

A zombie if you will

Survive day for the night

Surrendering to human needs

Innocently she goes on

Until the sun sinks once more

The immortal one rises

Sanity wilts to the floor

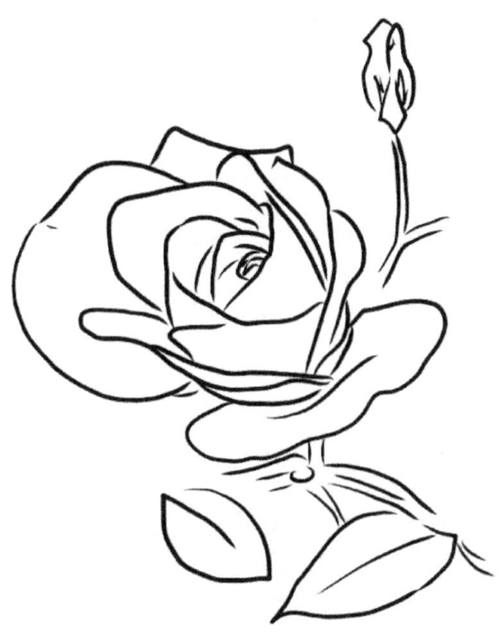

Rose 2022

## Untitled

Withered soul, ravaged hair

Bruised flesh, empty stare

What the fuck is wrong with you

Judging me as though I am defective

I can never do right in your eyes

I confuse you

You failed so many times

I am still breathing

You strained to destroy me

And enjoy the attempt

Tormenting, with sneers

Teasing and condescendence

Some days I am fragile

You catch me off guard

However I get stronger

Each day better than last

You reek of pathetic

I stand taller in repulsion

Is this jealousy?

Or are you that senseless

You dare destroy me?

You did that to yourself!

## Secret

Drifting silently through dark concrete forests

Night time creature of melancholy prognosis

Altered reflection since yesterday parting

Vanishing body of welcomed psychosis

Hollow craving in escape ambition

Numb from strength of torturous demolition

Mind, body, spirit departing

Resurrection intention through expert precision

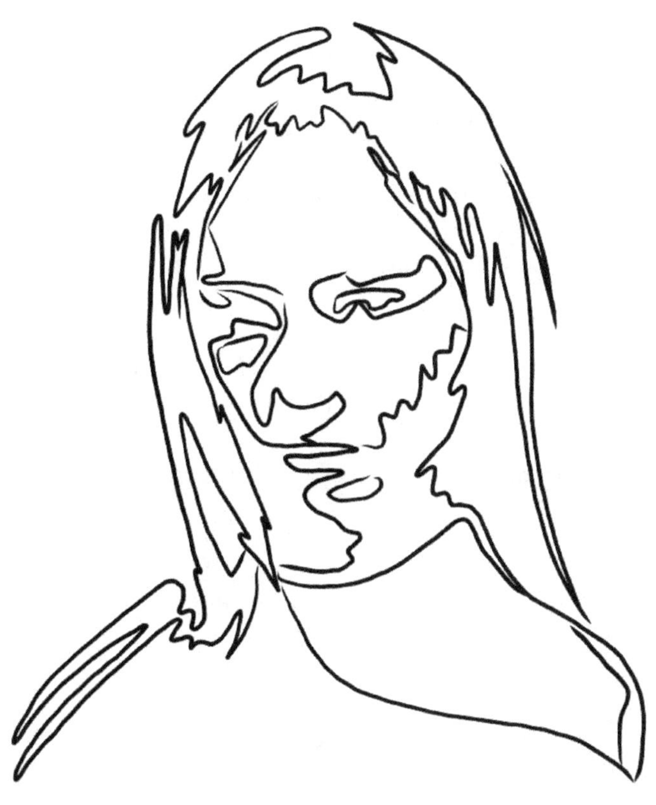

Resurrection

## The Staircase

Crying heart verses in sombre embrace

Paralysed and rooted, obscure in grace

Sleep they possess, unconscious above

Gradually withdrawing, love void of

Decay of dreams, fading within

Staircase dissociation, therein

A starvation of empathy, she's resolved to be silent

Avoiding the evils surrounding and violent

Stares through the wall of the staircase

She is but a waste of space

Stinging eyes, drought of tears

The Prophecies vacant, numb of fears

Madness proceeds, the child compliant

Ecstasy in her solitary confinement

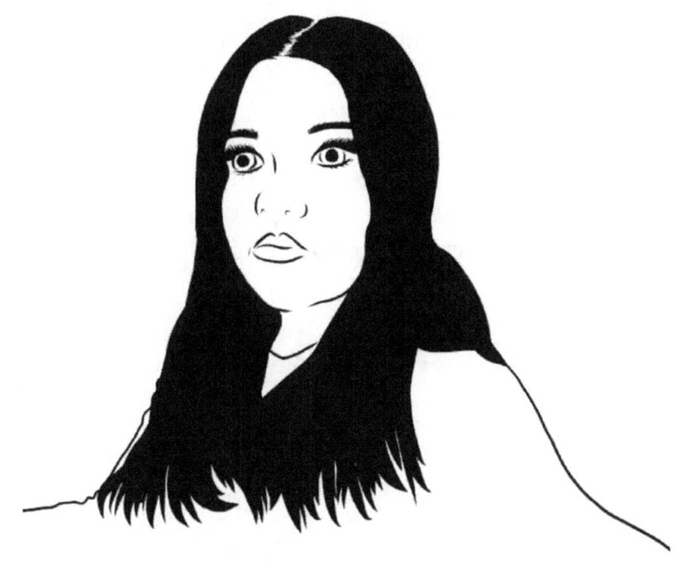

Staircase 2003

## Itch

Fingers gripping the highest branch,

Yearning to let go, weightlessness, freedom.

The trance of an uncontrollable impulse,

To relish in wakeful dreams.

I hunger to drop, I cannot release,

To the finale with concluding breath.

## Can't escape her

Do you know what they say about you?

I suppose you don't care

Do you think that they know you?

That I know you?

I see more than they do

I see more than most

Yet you still won't let me in

I don't really want to

I can't escape you

Try as I might

You try to destroy me

You try to destroy us

You destroy everything

But this one thing you can't touch

You know much I need him

You know he is my only reason for life

Reasons why you want to break him

To break us

To break me

## Things I can't say

Every day exactly the same

I screamed into the night for so many

They sucked the life out of me

You're the perfect disaster

And you think you're so special

You're insanely deluded

Every part of you

Destroying everything you touch

I cried for you, for too long

My legacy built from your empathy lacking

You like to make me feel helpless

You never gave a damn about me

What if I'm not there to give you attention?

If you actually gave a fuck tonight

I could never share the hell you caused

You would never understand what I gave up

I was strong for so long and held on to what?

All those who cared gave up on you

Congratulations, you finally pushed me too

No one gives a shit about you anymore

If only you knew the truth

I'm done

I was meant to live for so much more

Permission to not care

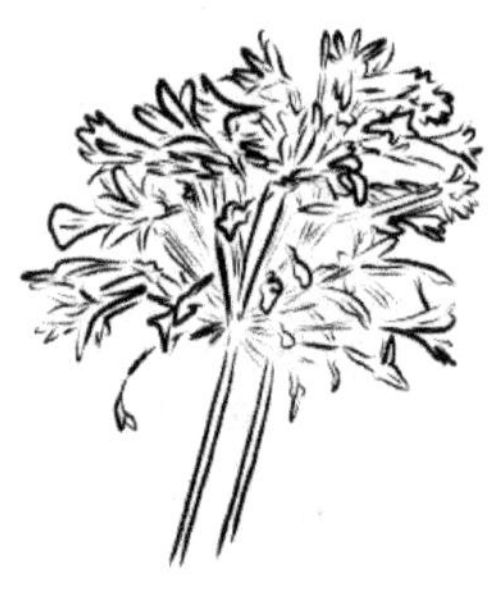

i

PART 2

# A Journey to Adulthood

## First Move

Summer night

White Pixie skirt

Salt in the breeze

Sand on our toes

My head on your chest

Your hand holding mine

The beat of our hearts

The curve of my spine

The sound of the ocean

Hot sweaty palm

Waiting for something

Strawberry lip balm

Trying to not breathe

Starting to shake

Blame the cold

Body ache

We

Lay

We

Wait

## First kiss

Holding hands,

Autumn nights.

Waves crash,

Star lights.

Air salty ,

Sky clear.

Cold Sand,

No fear.

Scene perfection,

Romantic bliss.

Nervous, yearning,

Impromptu first kiss.

# Untitled

Archaic compulsion for supremacy.

The transmogrified testosterone monstrosity,

Competing to feast,

Roams for the shiniest crown.

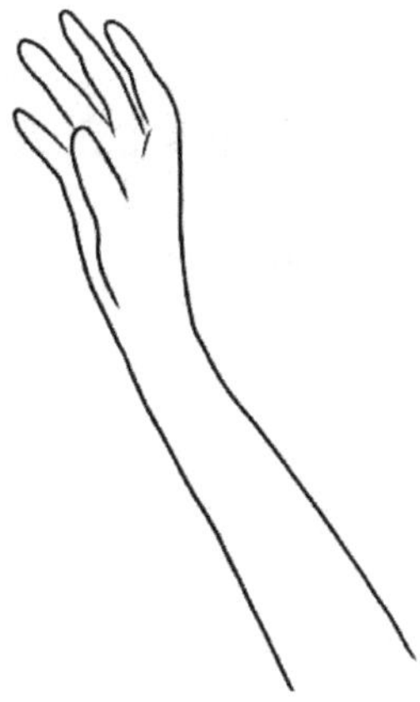

iii

## Pure Insanity 2004

I would watch the tap drip, as though it were rain.

I would nervously laugh with those in pain.

I'd make weird noises, and act such a fool.

I was confused; I was nice, mad, sad and cruel.

They told me where to go, strong meds, padded wall room.

Chained down and regressed to the womb.

You listened and cared, held my hand tight.

You guided and found me, and I found my knight.

## In this alone?

I will not liberate your morbid fantasies,

Yet I can't extirpate your atrocious dreams.

I will remain in tears, till my fears are absent.

For what is stronger?

Please let be your heart!

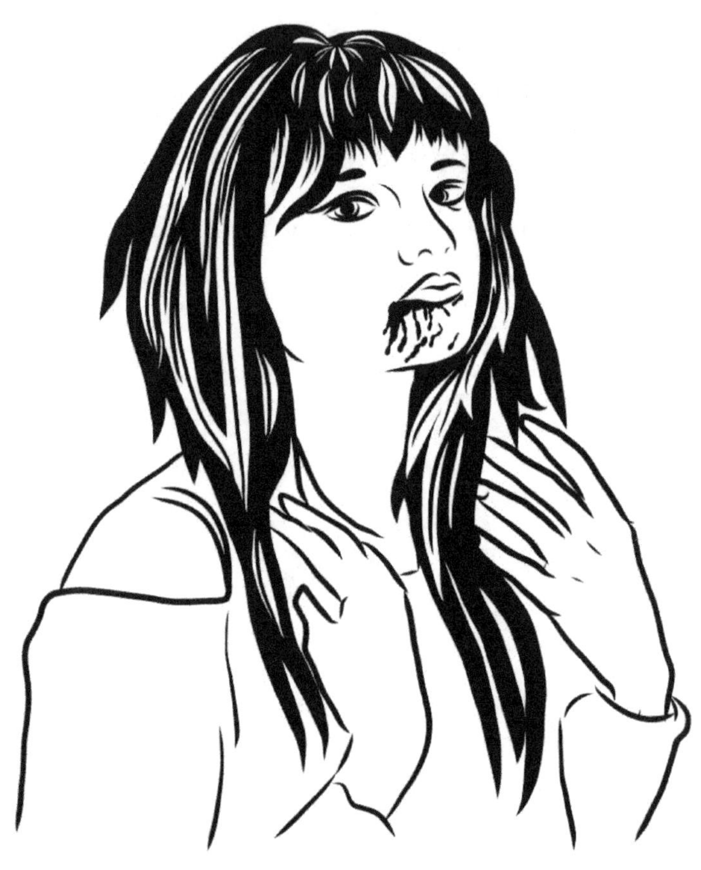

Desire

## Untitled

You welcomed me to your world

With your hopes and fucking dreams

Trying to make you happy by

Holding back my screams

You told me this is life

Manipulating me to abide

Blocking out my own wants and needs

Yet you say it's for me to decide

Oh will you let me think for once

Without the eye of must

Is it really a world of my love you seek?

Or your fucking world of lust

And can you hold back and understand

The do's and don'ts of my truth

And can you wait a little longer

To savour the ending of our youth

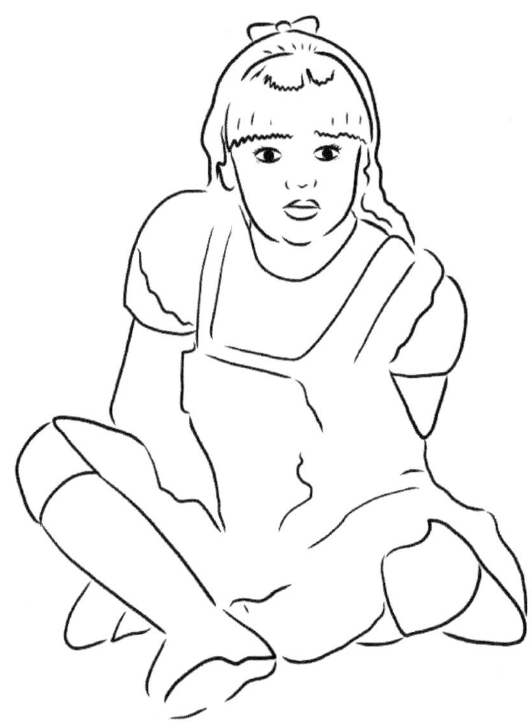

Youthful

## Piece

You tore me up like an unwanted letter

Erasing the words I had sworn by

Destroying my existence

Nothing more but an object

A fuckable live girl

My worth was confirmed

Fight or Flight

Defeated nonetheless

## Walking ghost

Ramblings of my soul, my truth

Innocent Immortal, lost youth

To live will be the greatest play

To die will be the easy way

Non-existence I crave foremost

Eternally till death, a walking ghost

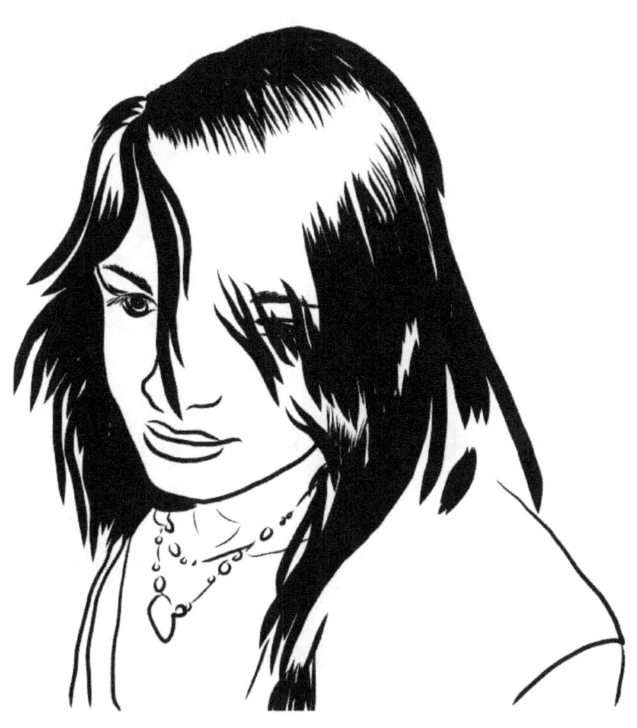

Eternal

## Complexity of the naive

If I had to explain

Id' nothing to say

You will always say I'm childish

Well I know,

There's nothing you can say to change me

This war of love, a plague

I am worthy of empathy

Or is empathy an obligation for humanity

I live to cast no shadow

Some would call it weak

I don't stand for the bullshit

It's all for show

I continue on my path

Bet it feels good when I let you pretend to care

What would they ask of you?

Draining the pain from you

Gaining more than sadness

We are just a trickle of time

The hardest part of existence

A collision of our passing

Yet I'm not good

I'll never be good

Terms I accept

But I will miss you

You'll never let me go

I loathe you, I need you

I want what I desire

Tragic Farewell

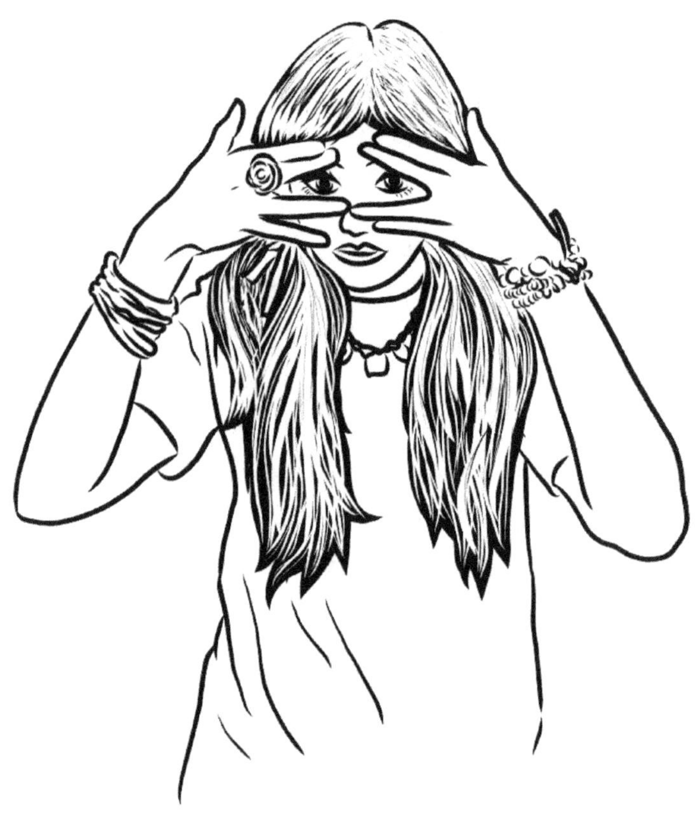

See 2003

## Not of value

I've had a taste of your dream,

You wanted so desperately to dive in.

Time has gone and I've felt the worst,

It can't be undone; long for it reversed.

Obscure Polaroid memory,

Of what I had and lost.

Stuck between the do or die,

Evident change, but what cost?

You think I am different, I am only more certain.

You think I should slave for you.

Things I should do, the things I should be,

That anything human is inconvenient to you,

You're so very disappointed in me.

I now believe you won't ever understand.

Im sorry I can't be that girl.

I guess this is Goodbye...


For an Angel in his world who still hasn't gained his wings.

From an Angel in her world who hasn't lost them...

To the end my tainted soul.

Tell me I matter

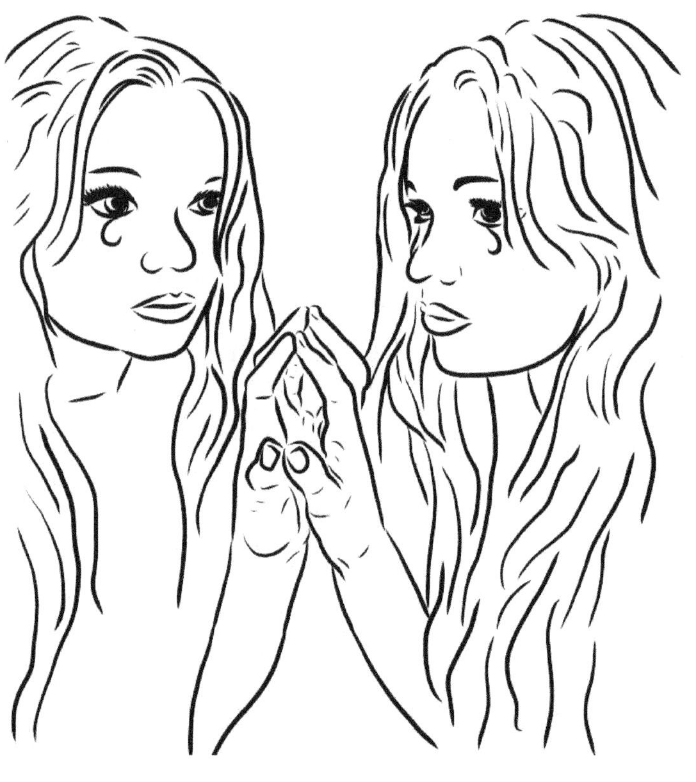

Mirror

## Characterless

When in tears

When in pain

When in fear I call one name

To him I call

His name through tears

Yet when I fall

He does not hear

Perhaps he did

He chose to ignore

The screams from me

Shaking on the floor

The pain increasing over me

Sucking me into a black hole of nothing

Dominating, draining, my soul, what's left of me

I reach for your hand, yet you turn away

All because I wouldn't let you stick your dick in.

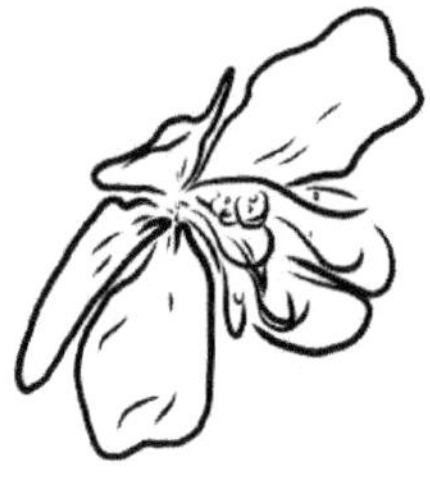

ii

## Scene

Hands down my pants

I tell him too far

He angrily stops

And sits there in silence

What did I do?

I've done it this time

He's going to leave me

I'll be alone again

He's all that I have

Sitting in silence

His hand slides in again

I sit there, frozen

I had already said no?

I don't want to upset him again.

48

What do I do?

His fingers slide in

I try not to cry

I sing a song in my head

Wake up, wake up

This is not you. Stop it now

I pull his hand out

I say no once again

Angrily he grunts

Silence again

Processing my thoughts

Why did I make him upset?

No, I won't do it

They say I can say No

Only minutes pass, his hand reaches again

Why is he doing this? I already said No!

I explain again, I'm not ready, please stop.

He stands up, "Why am I here then?"

"I am wasting my time."

I shed a tear as he walks out the door

The clear summer sky calling him

I follow behind him, hoping he will come back

He says good bye and doesn't look back

My heart is broken

I feel this is it

I turn to face my home

The dark from within

My fate is sealed; I belong in this haunted house

Of abuse and trauma

I cry myself to sleep

The next day, you act normal

You come over like nothing has changed

I realised I overreacted, you still love me, you are still my hero

Everything is great, listening to music and having fun

Then you start to undo my pants

I freeze,

Just focus on the music, I tell myself

Just let him do it, don't upset him again, he will leave you again

Just make him happy, it's not that much of a deal

Focus on the music. Focus on the music. Focus on the music

I never liked this song

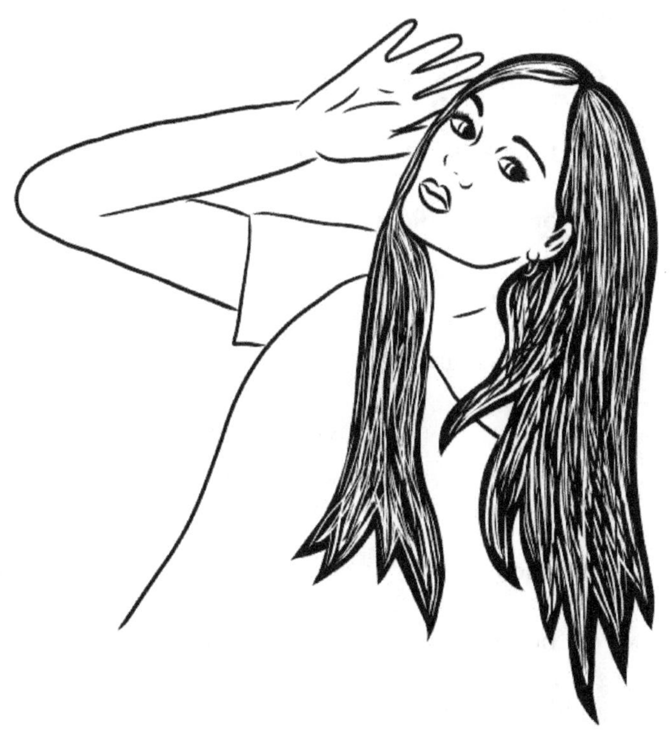

Flow

## War

Ruined the one chance I had of making him happy

I chose me over him

I tell myself he should be ok with it

It's not my problem

… Or maybe it is?

I should just give in.

They all say I should give him what he wants

Bloody people

Fuck them all

I cry because he is disappointed with me

I cry because I'm not ready

All I do is cry.

Maybe I should at least make one of us happy?

For the price of my tears

You can have it all

What a joke.

Why is the power in my hands?

I didn't ask for this.

Why can't you just be ok with it?

Why demand this of me?

Why do they tell me I'm selfish?

Why is his needs of using me more important?

Why do I care?

It is because I love him so.

I should give in… I should want to make him
happy
am I selfish for not wanting to have sex just yet?
I fear…

Losing the one last thing that meant importance
to me

The one thing you lived for

To give in, my life is over

Yet I fear it hasn't even begun

I suppose, why bother, I'm already dead inside

## That one time

Blooming as you descent from above

I dare query, yet my now consciousness does tell

Not blooming, fading,

You used me, without honour

To rise when I was ready,

To let be when it was time.

I voiced it loudly, daily; on the minute

Did you ever really listen?

Did you even think of me?

And even when you realised what you did,

You just rolled over and went to sleep.

While I frantically searched for meaning,

Trying to make it ok.

But it was not ok. I realised what was taken.

My choice, my dream.

And you sleep there, satisfied, back facing me

I so badly want to scream, to cry,

To make you experience the hurt I am feeling

To claw at your back to tear out your insides

Hysterically watch you laugh as I try and fail

Madness increasing as my anger takes over

I can't be here, I am nothing, and you obviously
see me as nothing

But I know you can never, and will never
understand

And why do I love you. I hate you so much right
now.

I want to vomit, I start to shake.

I leave the bed and run as fast as I can.

The dark air burning my throat

To the highway, and up the hill

I want to go home, I need to escape.

I stop… my tears are sticky

And my eyeliner is stinging.

I have nowhere to go

Nowhere to run

You are all I have.

You are my home.

I collapse to the concrete.

Graze my knees on the fall.

I pull at my hair and silently scream.

You have taken me, absorbed me

I have no one to care

I stand and I turn

I make my way back

I return to the bed,

I go back to you.

Nowhere to go,

I have nothing but you.

A shot to forget.

A shot for loss

A shot for the memory

A shot for a shot

Another for good luck

I go numb.

I sleep.

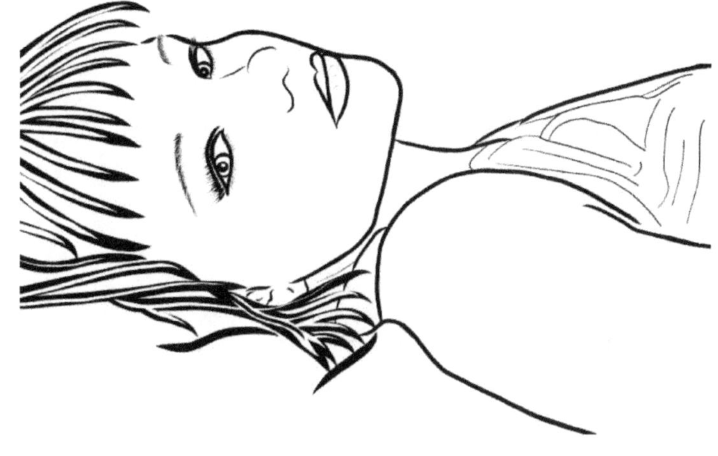

Numb

## Three Days

Three days,

Feels like forever since you were inside me

You are not here, but I can feel you

We have not spoken, and I cry

I sit on my bed, waiting for your affection

I am completely yours now

Three days,

I can't think for myself

I wait for you

Persevering

Three days

And I'm sickened

Of the power you now have over me

Three days,

Where are you? What did I do wrong?

Three days,

Nightmarish flashbacks of you on top of me

Three days,

Blistered feet and still shoeless

Three days,

Still nothing

Why won't you call?

Only three days

She must be broken?

## Pyromaniac

As you seek the hot wild light,

The passion and the flame.

The world around you vanishes,

And I become a game.

You use me like an object,

Caress me like a toy.

You look at me with lust,

And my heart you destroy.

Your eyes become much brighter,

Your heart then beats so fast.

The power of the flame has taken you,

And you return to me at last.

You kiss me with your eyes,

A thank you for my part.

And then you gently hold me,

And say I'm in your heart.

You leave with a smile,

As my body fills with black.

And as I see you walk away,

I wish for one glance back.

But it never happens,

It kills me more each day.

I beg of you please hold me longer,

Why is it this way?

PART 3

# Lost

Dreaming of a life not lived but
holding onto the fantasy because
scars of reality still sting the heart.

## I believe she is hormonal

Ramblings of a woman, deranged

Melancholy blood, feeding the veins

Moving the limbs

Innocently chained

Life embraces, yet people misuse it

Abuse it, ruin it, destroy all for self

Win or lose

In time it will mean nothing

The life I lead is not quite passing

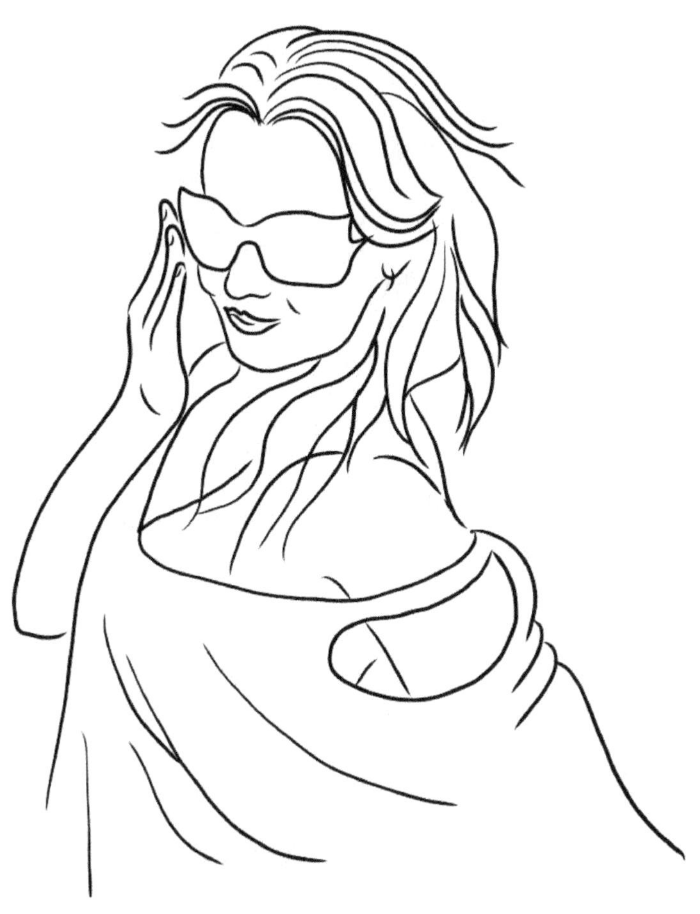

Pretender

## Fugue

Lost girl in a sea of strangers

The stench of mud and trampled grass

Music thumping, bodies jumping

Screaming riots, broken glass

Body odour mixed tobacco

Stale deodorant and booze

Vomit hills, video stills

Rampage for fame, stage dive views

My now empty hand

Once friendly with yours

I have no phone, perfectly alone

I search for a face I cannot recall

Go back to basics; I follow the horde

I forget who I am, I start to explore

Chains fall, climb the wall

Assume new identity, free forevermore

## Selective Insomnia

The bed retains nightmares

Of the dead I lay buried

Writhing in reanimation under the vomit stained sheets

I run my hand along the pillow

Fingers conducting in coagulated blood and dried vomit

Eyelids painfully lift like healing gashes of broken flesh

Stinging as they tear like the red sea parting

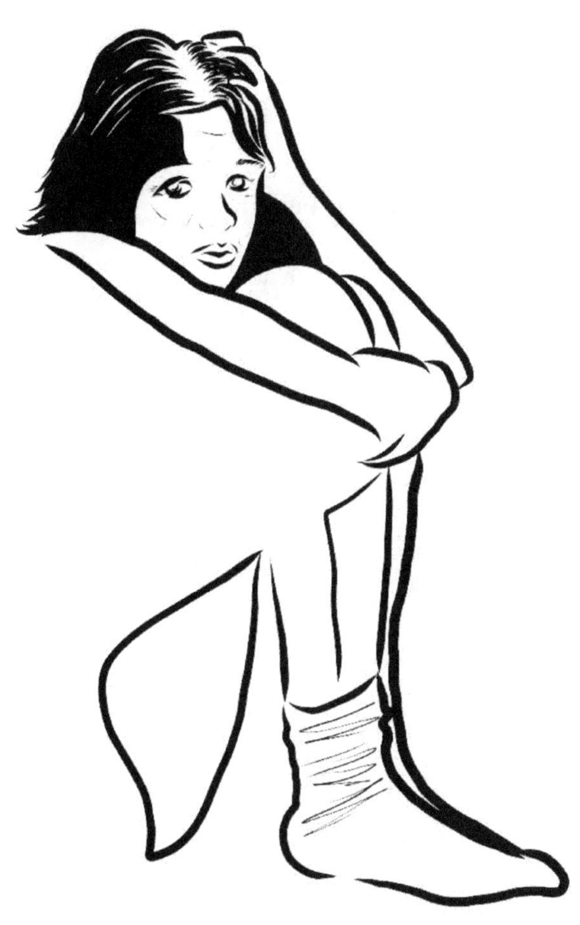

Insomnia

## Untitled

Flame flickers, sleep am I,

Fear vacant, embers fly.

Unbeknownst, stir not I,

Wax falls, Candle dies.

## Face Paint

Age three, so young,

I accepted the role of beautiful princess.

As most young girls do.

Everyone is a princess they promised,

I never felt like a princess,

Try as I might.

I'd see all the other princesses playing

While I struggled to say Hi..

Try harder they cheered.

You will fit right in.

I didn't understand them,

I felt Alien.


Mother was beautiful,

As most mothers are.

Putting on makeup, I desired to ask.

Why do you hide yourself?

She'd smile, so others can see my beauty.

Confusion, a feeling, I would learn to ignore,

Came strong today, more so than before.

I must paint my face, it's what beautiful people do,

To show that they are princesses,

I begged for paint too.

I painted my face, I did it myself.

We both got dressed up,

My confidence high,

Everyone will see the real me tonight.

My joy was short lived,

MY GOD they screamed in disgust
my soul crumpled,

I looked to my mother, please let it be flawed

I felt alone, in this new found rejection.

I noticed her anger, the tears in her eyes,

Doesn't she look beautiful she said through a strained smile.

I may have been young, but I knew something was wrong,

I wasn't beautiful with makeup,

I could never be a real princess,

I'd never belong.

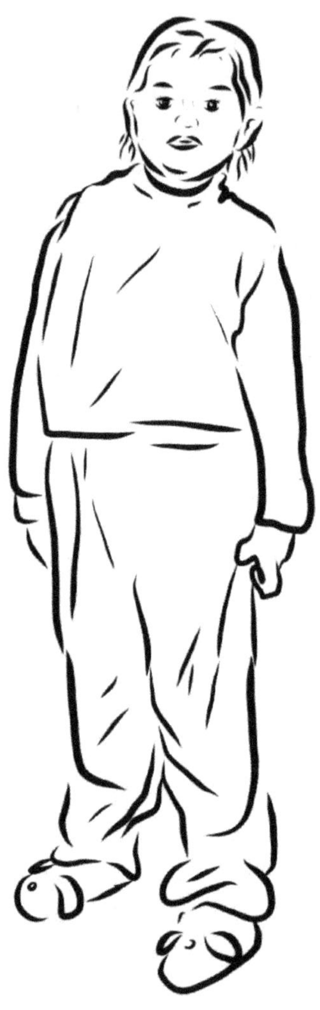

Anxiety at three

## Wasted Childhood

I was always a thinker,

Needed to understand why.

I wasn't like most children, asking why, why,
why.

I needed to know it, feel it and observe it.

A deep rooted prerequisite to my sanity,

My happiness and being.

I could never block it out, or shrug it off,

Get over it, they would say, you will grow out of
it they could promise.

I never did. I grew up with hatred, sadness and
more whys.

It appeared no one cared for my tears.

Just a child they said. Too young to know
sadness, fear and pain, they said.

I begged to understand, people, the world.

The cruelness of being.

You will understand one day they said, smile, and go play.

They never listened, didn't try to understand.

I only had me. Yet I felt I didn't have me, the world had Me, judged, taken, used and abused.

Without answers I retreated,

I hid from the pain.

Trying hard not to think, or experience more whys,

Away from the people, the hatred, the lies.

Even kindness was conceited,

I just wanted to be free,

If they refused answers,

I'd have to think through them myself.

They took that away too. Go outside and play.

. . .

And as I got older,

A shift in reaction,

It's too late for me.

They shake their head with a tsk.

"I should know better"

Confusion.

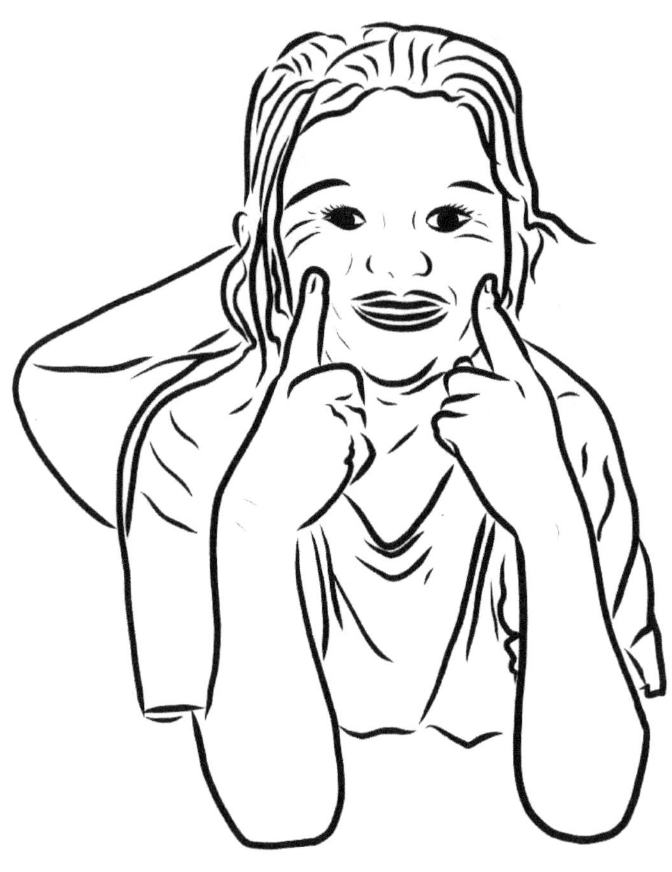

Smile

# Love

You used to feel entitled to have a woman's
body,

You couldn't understand why I wouldn't slave
for you

Is this what is expected?

Am I broken?

The funny thing is now you have given me your
heart completely,

I am entirely your slave.

## She died

My oh my, I loved you so,

My childish dreams, my innocent vulnerability,

You never listened, did you even care?

Today I muse over those early days of us,

My morals and wishes seem so insignificant now,

But to a child it was the ultimate end.

To be pure until I was ready,

I thought I could control.

I couldn't stop people staring,

Daydreaming, or fantasizing.

No matter how hard I hated it,

No matter how hard I tried to make it stop.

I felt so young, sex wasn't appealing.

Yet no matter how often I'd say no,

You would threaten to leave me,

Look at me like you were upset with me.

Torment me with silence,

And then try again, and again, and again.

Over time you had me beaten,

I would just let it happen and block it all out.

Just let him touch you, he will love you if you do.

It tortured me, yet you never understood,

You thought I could be conquered, like times before

My first time, I wanted to be on my terms.

MY TERMS. That's all I had left.

You took that too.

## Interlude

Interesting thoughts of trying to find my identity and make sense of my emotions:

I fall through the floor, without a given warning. The membrane of floor ruptures, and slowly I sink along with the thick sultry amniotic fluid which gushes over as gravity takes me. The further I descend the more open, cold and empty the space becomes.

Through fear, I look for help, or something to hold on to. Yet I fail to raise my hand. A fear of rejection has reduced me to immobility. I find a sense of acceptance in my fate. It's too late for help even if I could fight.

I'm at least ten feet down when my feet quietly and softly hit the ground. I land on dark empty floors so cold it stings the skin of my feet like shards of glass. Again, I have no will to fight.

The pain in the soles of my feet shoot up through my legs like electric tremors.

I look up to the people now above me, continuing on with their day. They don't realise I have disappeared from sight. Did they even know I was there to begin with? Even for a moment? Do I even exist to them? Would I ever exist to anyone? Like ants in a nest, is this all it is. Do I even exist at all?

I shake myself, "wake up, you pathetic girl." Stop feeling worthless. It is not right. You are mistaken in your confused emotions. The people just can't see, they are blinded by their ways. All humans are selfish, self-entitled; they only want you as an accessory, or not at all. If they choose to help, they are only doing it for themselves anyway. They don't care; they never have, and never will. They cannot care at all.

The emptiness closes in again… the darkness compressing my body and suffocating my veins.

You fade into the scenery, with nothing to do or say. Just get on with the day, like you are the extra in a movie. You are to be as they want you to be. Follow the script.

Release.

The ground once again begins to quake. Before I can look down to see what will be, I fall once more. I have fallen so far I cannot make out the walls, and only darkness can be seen below me. I look up, to see a watery like ceiling, lighted by the daylight. I can just make out the movements of people walking above, oblivious to what is happening below their feet. Even if I could, I see no way of exit, and now that I look deeply, I see no sign of my entry either.

Faces blurred, above me, fading as I descend… The speed of my falling increases, yet I can't accurately tell how fast I am going now, it all feels the same. The ceiling appears to be closing in; the light above me grows more distant. I can no longer see signs of life. I scream out...

Nothing...

The dreaded feeling has come to feel like home now. I feel safe in this paralysed descent into nothingness.

Relax.

Falling again, further from reality, further from the living. My breathing is calm, my heart rate is resting. I smile. I am ok with this situation. This is my survival. I have done this many times before. I become the invisible observer. No longer do I fear the public perception of my words and thoughts; my actions and motives. No longer do I see myself playing in the minds and eyes of others. I am at peace with my fate and I am at war, only with the fact it took me so long to accept it.

Peace.

Euphoria is short lived. Something warm grabs hold of my ankles. Like a snake, or a vine; it is strong, and it is scorching my skin. It twists itself around my waist… I find a new strength within myself. I am annoyed at my disturbed peace, and I am angry at this thing trying so hard to destroy me. I decide to fight it. While it blisters my skin, I grip at it tightly, and try to pull it off my skin. I struggle as it grips tighter and tighter. I silently scream out in pain, realising I can feel the circulation of my blood getting cut off.
Another vine wraps around my arms… the pain floods in as it did before. I cannot move. Burning my skin as it glides over my bare skin and tightening its grip around me. I start to panic. How dare this thing ruin the peace I had found within my misery?
Another vine, and then another, they come out from all directions, I can't see where they originate from. They are snatching at me, holding me, contorting my body to positions

they want of me. I fight so hard to open my mouth to scream, but still, no sound is released. It does not emotionally upset me. What use will it be to draw any attention to myself anyway? No one knows I am here. I am nothing. Remember. A worthless nothing. I shouldn't have been up there, and I shouldn't even be here; I am ruining everything for everyone by existing. Again, as before, I relax. My breathing slows, and I ease my activated muscles. I stop fighting the pain, and give into it. I allow the vines to glide over me, choke me, penetrate me; I focus on relaxing. I focus on breathing. I ignore the pain of the vines. I ignore them entirely. I become their energy source, slowly sucking what it left of my existence. My soul slowly decays. So be it.

# Interlude 2

I'm not aware how long I was in darkness, not aware when the vines chose to lose grip. The first thing I noticed was a light above me. Slowly increasing in size as I slowly ascended the obscure cave of darkness. Floating like a balloon and emotionally lost in acceptance of surrender. I reach the surface of earth, and climb out of the now small entrance of the dark hell I somehow escaped from. Back to life, back to reality. With no energy to rise, I look around at the people rushing around me, ignoring my re-entry into life. Looking a mess, I continue to sit on the pavement, watching the people around me go about their day. Eyes refusing to acknowledge and hearts refusing to care. Realizing, the land of the vines was much more tolerable than this place.

I am one fucked up soul!

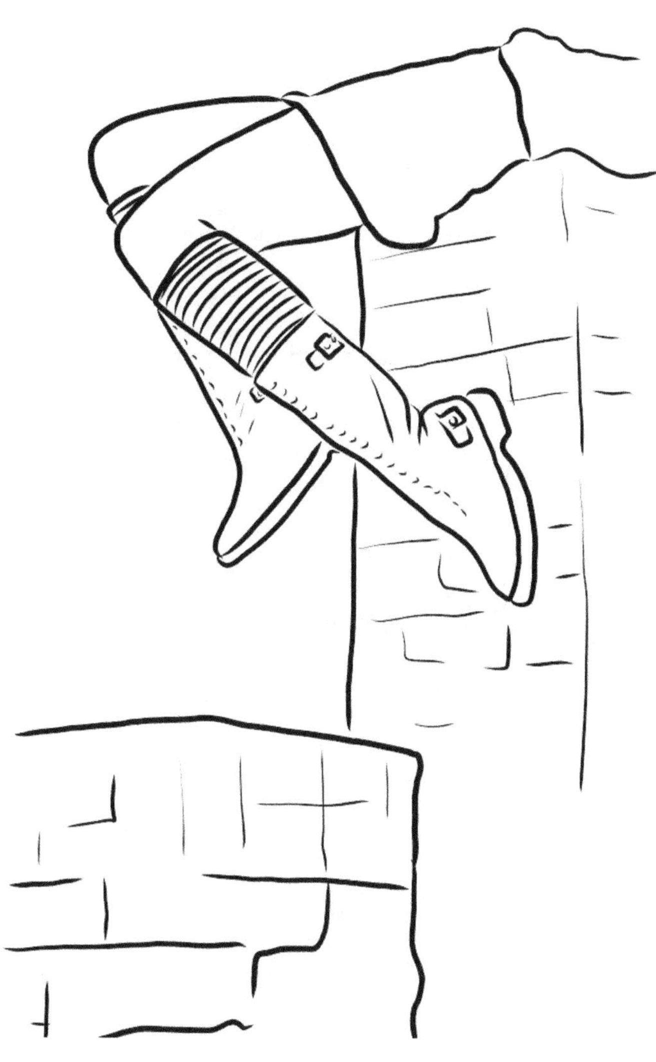

Falling

## Bipolar Liquid

The crisp bite of your papercut arch

Seducing like a puppeteer manipulating my
humanity

Starved by the dehydration of loneliness

I crave a taste of the warm glacier of bitter lip
wounds

Stung by the elixir of bipolar liquid

Staining the album of history

Destroying life once more

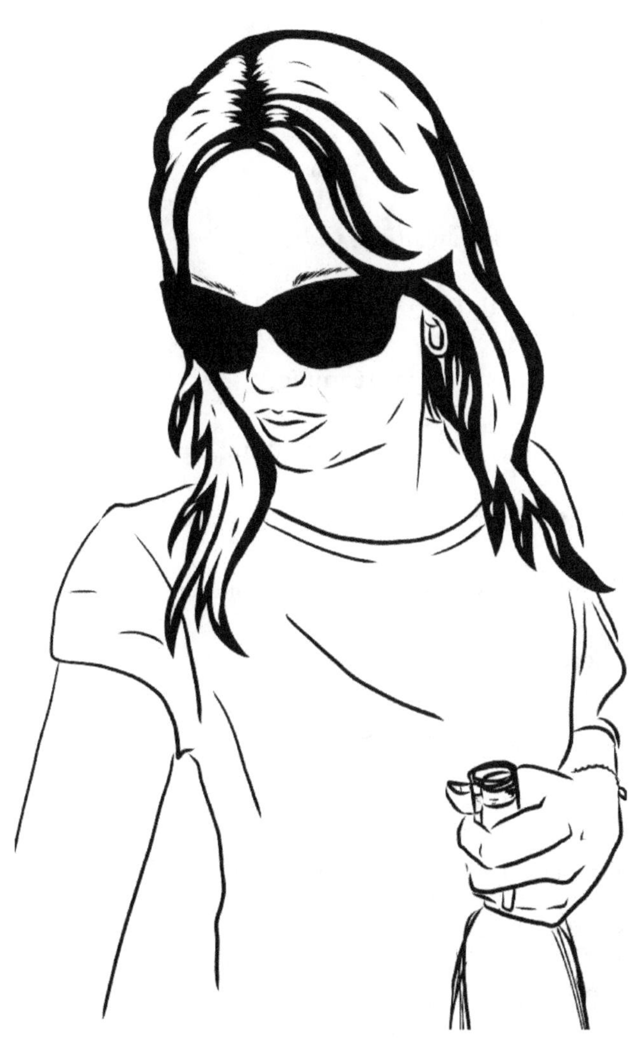

'Wine time'

## Wasted

Slowly clawing at my veins

Days, weeks, awaiting, yearning

I am spared, I am surrendered

Body aches, body screaming,

Body cries, a need for something,

What's wrong with me?

Where is the hunger? Am I Broken?

I scream I cry no one dare hear me

Wasted space, wasted time…

I'm worth nothing; I resolve to be a nothing

I'm fighting so hard, to wanting and being
nothing

Nothing at all

## Untitled

Immortality ascending

Elixir spill of dream

Craving, Needing, Breathing

Banshee screeching scream.

Away with the fairies

Toadstool circle slave

Dancing with the Goblins

Mornings, Nights, to the grave

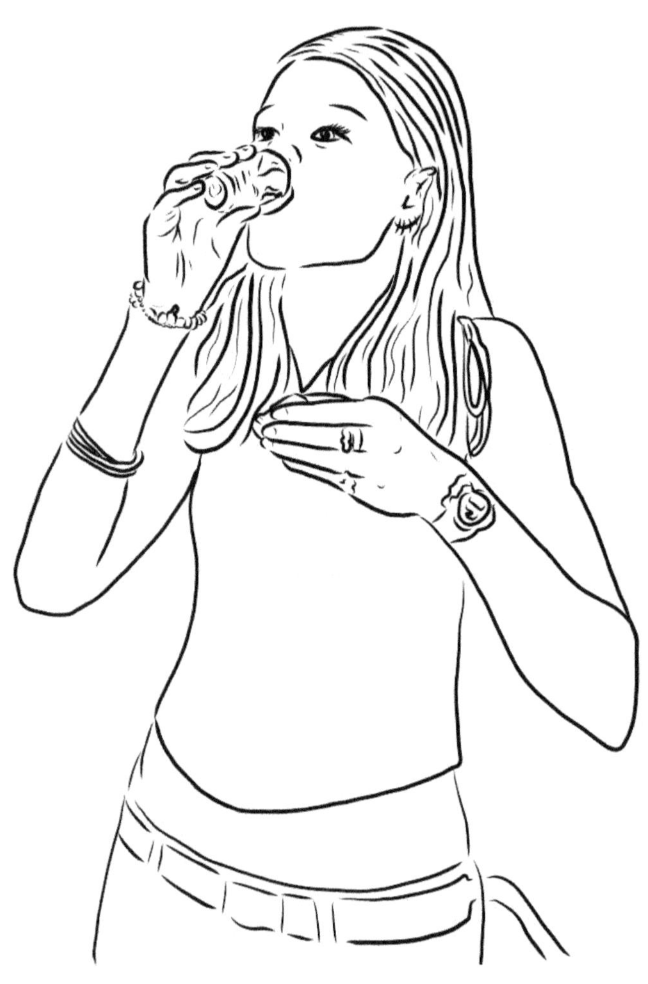

Depression

## Succumb

Most days you rise and start to fade…

With each day I decay, accepting the inevitable fact, that the world is fucked.

## Without you

I am split and my sanity is gone

Without you I am nothing

Without you I'm lost

I crave for resurrection

I need you to survive

Please stay with me always

Without you I am nothing

Without you I'll die

Tears all but fall

My face swells and aches

Monotonous wandering

Until you return

Nothing without you

## Only Human

Edging closer to the cliff

You didn't seem to notice

Empty bottles, weeping veins

Collapse in you when the flood runs

The noose around my neck

Tight embrace of my breath

Heart aggressive

Trying to restart

I feel me falling

Falling so fast

Falling, falling

Falling apart

Body aching screaming for relief

Soul torn

Shredded canvas

You don't deserve this, none of you do

I should go, I'm nothing honestly

Don't dare ache for me

I'm always broken

Always in pain

A change of heart, I try to stand

Break apart, hold out my hand

Come, come, take me home

I'm trembling, hysterically

Aching for a new start

Dream of hanging from a tree

Bury me if you care to

How'd I ever end up here?

A pill, a bottle? A rope?

Fated to this way of being

Feet never touching the ground

You drag me to my knees

Tell me straight through broken tears

Do or die, for we still need you

Hold me tight and shake me so

My love will never fade

Battle for victorious control

Over ourselves

# Cycles

Drowning the Vein

Wave of warm

A loving hug

Calm the storm

Happy tingle

Floating on air

Dizzy spells

Nothing to care

Getting worse

Fall to the floor

Pick up the bottle

Down some more

Hope to fade

Never to rise

Oblivion dream

Bottles, bottles, bottles, lies

Wake again

Flooding tears

Remedy reach

Monsoon tears

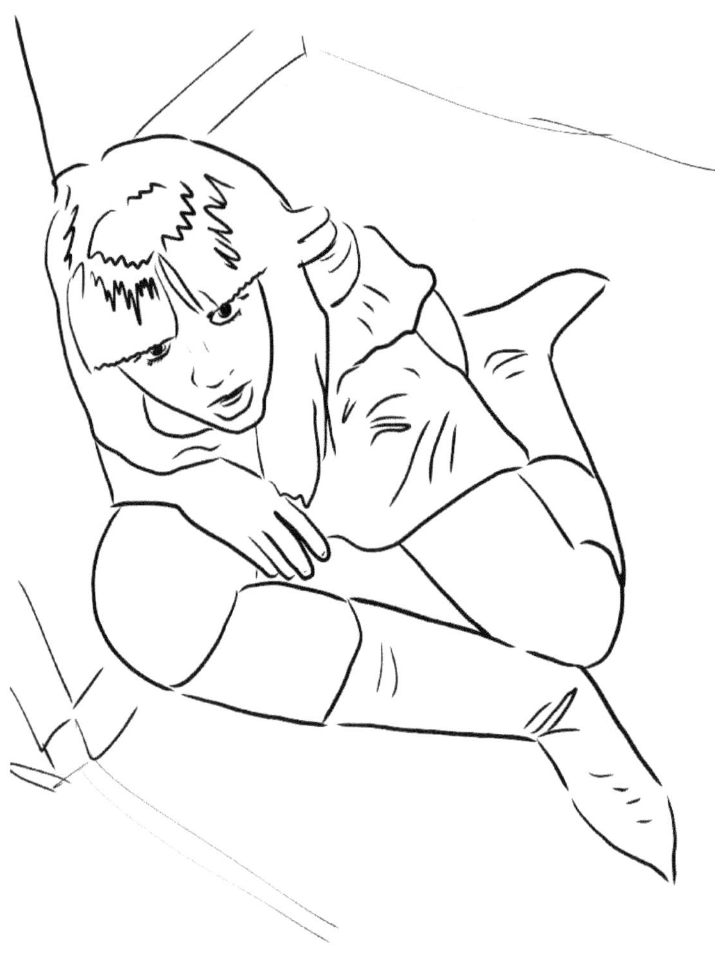

Floor

## Twenty One

Is this the way of life?

Nothing here seems real

Every night the same predictable scene

Stage set like an autopsy performance

Assured I died years ago

My body, nothing but a reanimated mess

Combating the inevitable deterioration

Fatigued

I don't want to play anymore

Leave me, let me rest in peace

-Alcohol, sweet release

## Possessed

Eyes tracing the foetal contour

Of vomit stained sheets.

Chronicles of dancing and

Violent tantrums

The room is vacant

But for a silhouette memory

She howls from the past

I weep from the nightmares

Through thunderous silence

Imitating the ghost

Trapped and broken

Lay down on her shape

I fight to consume her

To devour her energy

To heal her wounds

Yet I fail

Motionless she paralyses

Absorbs my body,

Manipulates my consciousness

Possessed

I struggle to rise

I struggle to think,

Trapped and Latent

I become her

She becomes me

Again

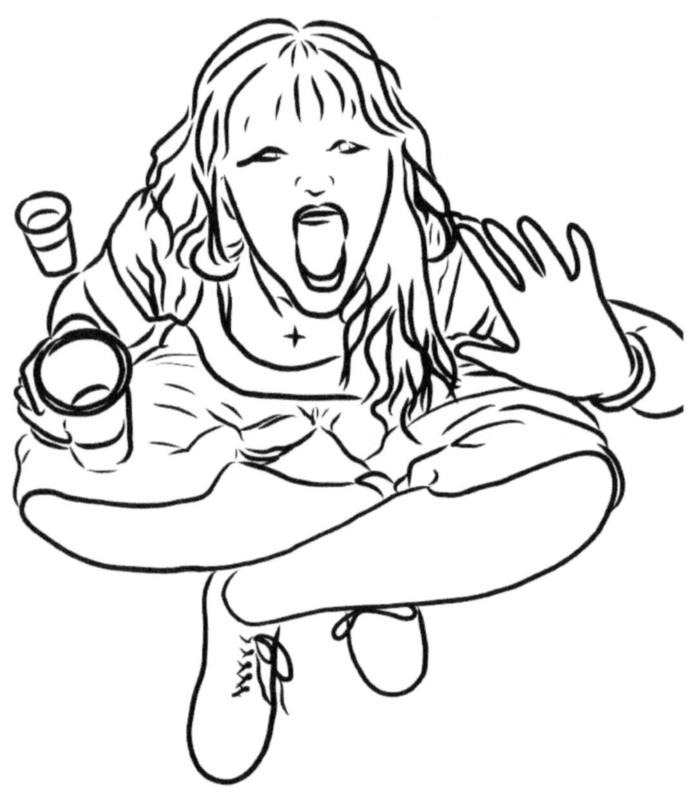

Banshee

## Funeral

The perspiration of shock romance,

Drowns the spirit like a hymn of sorrow.

Painting my mortal suit,

Washing away my ultimate dream.

## Photographic Memories

Shaken for clarity
A rousing of truth
Prominent in portraits of
Vacant eyed youth

PART 4

# SO FORTH

*Happiness is radiating*

112

## Fifteen years

Fifteen years believing it was my fault

Fifteen years blaming myself

I shouldn't have drank

Shouldn't have teased

Shouldn't have held off and just let him in

Shouldn't have cared so much

Should've been a good girl

Should've agreed

I shouldn't complain

I shouldn't cry

I shouldn't make him sad

Can't tell anyone

Can't say his name

Well Fifteen years is up

And I still hurt from the pain

I can no longer make excuses

They only mask the trauma

Because if I was guilty

I wouldn't still feel this way

114

## Trigger

Devoid of notice

I regress to those years

I give in to the emotions

I dive into old fears

Every step I take forward

I find strength in my growth

Today I'm still fighting

These poems my oath

Some steps are impossible

Sometimes I step back

I continue on forward

Creating a new track

Apologies and forgiveness

Won't dare touch my heart

But to share how I feel

Is a bloody good start

# Bright Side

A captive of emotions

Diaries enslaved

Evolution through dissection

Resolution paved

# Radiance

The peanut smell of your skin

Spells me to slumber like the glow of the worm

on an autumn evening

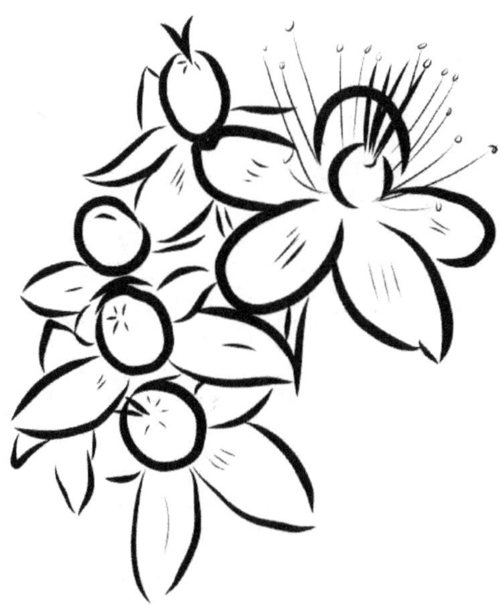

Flower Power

## Meditation

Summer sky,

Morning fog tone.

Quiet, peace, tranquillity,

Walking happy, alone.

Walking to nowhere,

Follow the sun.

Awakening, rising,

Start to run.

Running to nowhere,

Fresh air surround.

Heart beating,

Feet pound.

Going nowhere,

Escaping the past.

Collapse to the ground,

Mind slowing as last.

Mind going nowhere,

One deep sigh.

Lay for the view,

Summer sky.

## Lovers

From the time we connected

Oblivious to the end

Realising my pain and hurt

Meant losing my only friend

Days and Months passing by

Gradually tears ascending

What we gained now have lost

Lovers... The bitter ending

## Spring

Flowers enthusiastically smiling at the sun,

Freedom and curiosity

Young love and endless dreams

Scorned by the pessimism of aging oaks

Shading the growth suffocating the young

Insects raging war, weeds enveloping in
tournament

He loves me, He loves me not.

The garden screams to destroy

The flowers wilt and fade

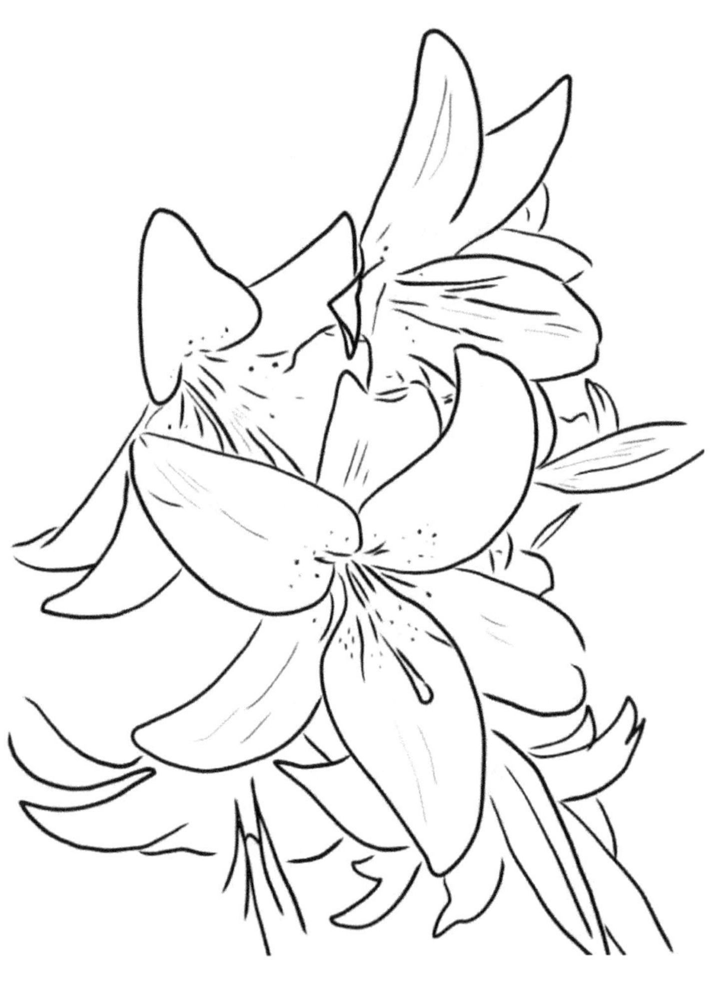

Yellow

## Soulmate

I first saw you under the moonlight

Our eyes locked, our souls embraced.

Destined for forever, together as whole

I loved you with my everything

You would run away from your prison to join me
in mine

Together we were invincible, together we were
extraordinary

They said we were too young, they didn't see you
were my hero

Or me as yours

We breathed each other, we saved each other

All we need is each other

To grow old, and die with you would be the
greatest gift

Together forever, my darling

## Better Now

Strolling through the written memories

A mosh pit of confusion

The massacre of youth

I was destroyed endlessly

By the broken

Petrified of loneliness

With a passion to help

Tolerated abuse while defeated

"You should smile more"

Never ending cycle of torment

They say they loved me

Few truly did

I questioned it

Unaccustomed to people's empathy

Unfamiliar to the cruelty

Yet the world moved on

I could not

The opportunity slain

I was not experienced enough to

"Get over it"

The loves I lost and the few who still stand

For those who never cared

To those who ignored it

To those who blamed me

And to those who never saw it

The pain was too real

Took years to rebuild

I am better now

## About Katri Maree

Katri Maree was born and raised in Australia, where she continues to live with her husband and 4 children. From a young age, she developed an interest in mental health, human behaviour, the human experience and storytelling through creativity. She completed a degree in Behaviour at University and studied Fine Arts, Graphic design, Photography and Makeup artistry. During her spare time she pursues creative endeavours, researching genealogy, dancing, exercising and studying current interests.